EXPLORE

ATOMS AND MOLECULES!

Silver 47

Ag

107.8682

Janet Slingerland

Illustrated by Matt Aucoin

ATOM

Molecules

More science titles in the **Explore Your World!** Series

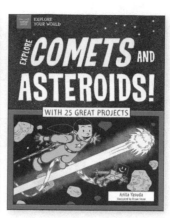

Check out more titles at www.nomadpress.net

Nomad Press
A division of Nomad Communications
10 9 8 7 6 5 4 3

ISBN Softcover: 978-1-61930-495-6
ISBN Hardcover: 978-1-61930-491-8

Educational Consultant, Marla Conn

Questions regarding the ordering of this book should be addressed to
Nomad Press
2456 Christian St.
White River Junction, VT 05001
www.nomadpress.net

CONTENTS

PS **Interested in primary sources? Look for this icon.**

Use a smartphone or tablet app to scan the QR code and explore more!
You can find a list of URLs on the Resources page.

If the QR code doesn't work, try searching the Internet with
the Keyword Prompts to find other helpful sources.

KEYWORD PROMPTS

atoms and molecules 🔍

CIRCA 500 BCE: The ancient Greeks propose the idea that atoms are the smallest pieces of matter in the universe.

1913: Henry Moseley proves an element's identity is defined by the number of protons it has. He rearranged the periodic table based on numbers of protons (the atomic number).

1669: Hennig Brand discovers phosphorus.

1913: Niels Bohr refines the Rutherford atomic model, introducing electron orbitals.

1911: Ernest Rutherford proposes a new atomic model where electrons orbit the nucleus like planets orbit a sun.

1808: John Dalton publishes his atomic theory, which includes the idea that all atoms in an element are the same and each type of atom has a unique weight.

1898: Pierre and Marie Curie discover the radioactive elements radium and polonium.

1869: Dmitri Mendeleev publishes the periodic table of elements.

1890s: J.J. Thomson discovers the electron, proving the existence of subatomic particles.

1896: Henri Becquerel discovers radioactivity.

1916: Gilbert N. Lewis devises dot structures as a way to show interactions between atoms.

2016: The names and symbols of the last four elements to be discovered are officially assigned and added to the periodic table. Element 113 becomes Nihonium (Nh), element 115 becomes Moscovium (Mc); element 117 becomes Tennessine (Ts), and element 118 becomes Oganesson (Og).

1917: Ernest Rutherford splits an atom, changing nitrogen into oxygen. In the process, he discovers the proton.

2011: Swiss scientists create PG5, the largest manmade molecule.

2004: Andre Geim and Konstantin Novoselov discover graphene, a form of carbon consisting of a single sheet of atoms. They were awarded the 2010 Nobel Prize in Physics for this discovery.

1932: James Chadwick detects neutrons and measures their mass.

1981: Invention of the scanning tunneling microscope makes it possible to view atoms and molecules.

1985: Robert Curl, Harold Kroto, and Richard Smalley discover ball-shaped forms of carbon called fullerenes. They win the 1996 Nobel Prize in Chemistry for their work.

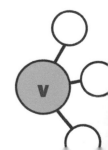

v

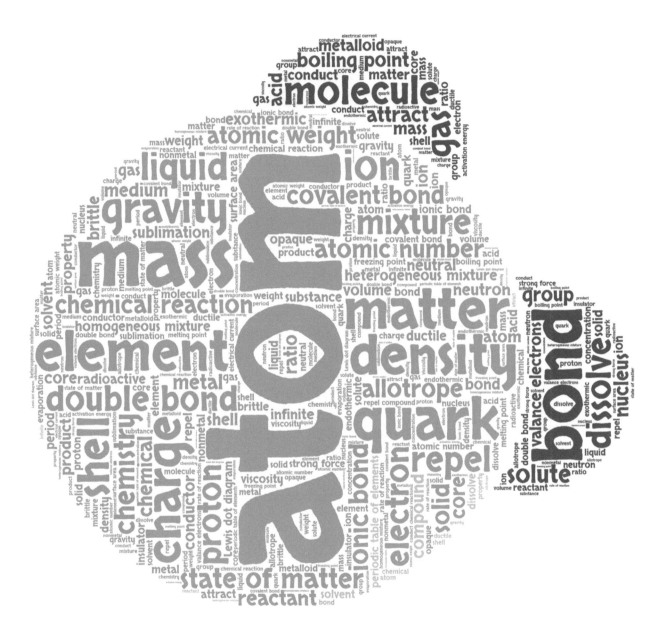

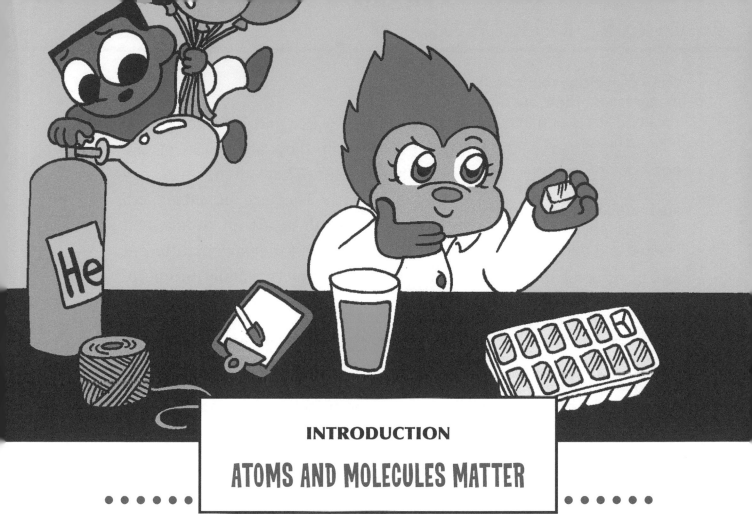

ATOMS AND MOLECULES MATTER

Atoms **and** molecules **are too tiny for people to see without using microscopes. If they're so small, why do they matter? They matter because they make up** matter, **which makes up everything around us.**

Matter is everywhere. It is the floor beneath your feet, the water in your glass, and the breeze in the air. Matter is anything that takes up space. Everything you can see, smell, and touch is made of matter. And all that matter is made of atoms and molecules.

WORDS TO KNOW

atom: a very small piece of matter. Atoms are the tiny building blocks that make up everything in the universe.

molecule: the smallest amount of something, made of atoms bound together.

matter: anything that takes up space.

1

state of matter: the form that matter takes. There are three common states of matter: solid, liquid, and gas.

solid: one of the three states of matter. The particles in a solid are bound together tightly. A solid has a definite shape and volume and does not flow.

liquid: one of the three states of matter. The particles in a liquid cluster together and flow. A liquid has a fixed volume and takes the shape of its container.

gas: one of the three states of matter. The particles in a gas are not bound to each other and move very fast in all directions. A gas does not have a definite shape or volume.

volume: the amount of space an object takes up.

mass: the amount of material that an object contains.

WORDS TO KNOW

Floors, water, and wind don't seem as though they are made of the same stuff. They all behave very differently. They are all matter, and they are all made of atoms and molecules. But they are in different states. Matter is usually in one of three states—solid, liquid, or gas.

STATES OF MATTER

A floor is solid. You can walk on it. You can jump on it. You can pile furniture on top of it. It doesn't easily change shape. You can even move it, with a lot of effort! You can cut it up into lots of pieces. Even in pieces, it is still floor.

Solids keep their volume. Volume is the measure of how much space an object takes up. Mass is the measure of how much matter fills that space.

Imagine a bowling ball and a soccer ball. Both balls are roughly the same size. They take up about the same amount of space. They have similar volumes.

2

GRAVITY

On Earth, gravity pulls an object toward Earth. Every planet has its own amount of gravity. There is less gravity on the moon than on Earth. A bowling ball that weighs 16 pounds on Earth weighs only 2.6 pounds on the moon because there is less gravity on the moon. The mass of the ball is the same on Earth as it is on the moon, though.

Do you want to know what you would weigh on other planets? **Find out at this website!**

KEYWORD PROMPTS

weight on other worlds 🔍 ← ─ ─ ┘

Now, imagine lifting both balls. Which is heavier? A bowling ball can weigh up to 16 pounds. A soccer ball only weighs about 1 pound. A soccer ball weighs less than a bowling ball. A soccer ball also has less mass than a bowling ball. But weight is a little different from mass. Weight measures how gravity acts on an object.

A floor broken into pieces takes up the same amount of space as the whole floor. A pile of floor pieces might seem bigger. This is because there is air filling the spaces between the floor bits. If you put the pieces back together, you could create the whole floor again and the size wouldn't change. The volume is always the same.

3

substance: matter, the material that something is made of.

WORDS TO KNOW

Water is a liquid. It pours easily from one place to another. You can fill a glass with it, pour it into a bowl, or make a water balloon with it. Liquid takes the shape of its container. Whatever shape it's in, the volume of the liquid stays the same. It takes up the same amount of space, even as it changes shape.

Gases float and change to fill the space they are in. Gas can be trapped in containers. Have you ever played with a balloon filled with helium gas? When balloons are filled with helium, they float. After a while, the gas slowly leaks out of the balloon and into the air. The balloon shrinks and sinks. Unlike solids and liquids, gases change in volume very easily.

BREAKING DOWN MATTER

What happens if you smash a piece of chalk with a rock? What if you keep pounding on the chalk? Eventually, all you would have is a pile of powder.

Imagine you could do this with any substance. You could cut it in half again and again. If you broke it apart enough, you would get to the smallest piece of a substance. This is a molecule.

Molecules can be split even further. Molecules are made up of atoms. Atoms are the smallest pieces of matter. They are far too tiny to see without a special kind of microscope.

Did You Know?

The word *atom* was first used thousands of years ago in Greece. It comes from the Greek word *atomos*, which means "that which cannot be split."

Have you ever looked at a sandy beach? It might be white or tan or even pink! From far away, it looks like a solid mass.

Then, when you step on the beach, it shifts under your feet. You can pick up a handful of sand and let the grains run through your fingers.

palette: a board used by a painter for layering and mixing paint colors.

pointillism: a style of art that uses tiny dots of color to create an image.

WORDS TO KNOW

GET THE POINT

In the late 1800s, an artist named George Seurat created a new art style. Most painters used only brush strokes to color their creations. Seurat used tiny dots of paint. He didn't even mix the paint colors on his **palette**. Up close, you can see all the tiny dots. Far away, it looks solid. The different-colored dots appear to form new colors. Seurat's new style was called **pointillism**. It works much like molecules do. Objects appear to be one mass. If you could zoom in really close, you'd see they're really made up of lots of tiny molecules.

Matter is similar to a beach. A solid object looks like it is just one thing. In reality, it is made of billions of atoms and molecules. One grain of sand is tiny. An atom is even smaller. One grain of sand contains millions and millions of atoms!

Why isn't all matter the same if it is all made up of atoms? Molasses and water are both liquids, but one is dark and the other is clear. Molasses pours very slowly. Water flows easily. Yet both are made up of atoms. They're different because the atoms that make up the two liquids are different.

WHY SHOULD YOU NEVER TRUST AN ATOM? *Because it makes up everything!*

All atoms have the same basic structure but with slight variations. Atoms are similar to letters. Letters make up a language. The letters all have the same purpose—to build words. They each have a slightly different shape, which tells us what sound they make. The letters "C," "A," and "T" make a very different word than the letters "J," "U," and "G." Atoms, too, are all a little different and they combine to form very different matter.

IT'S ELEMENTAL!

The **periodic table** of elements organizes all the known elements. An element is a substance whose atoms are all the same. Oxygen is an element. Oxygen gas is in the air we breathe.

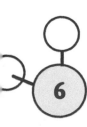

PERIODIC TABLE OF ELEMENTS

1 **H** hydrogen 1.0079																	2 **He** helium 4.0026
3 **Li** lithium 6.941	4 **Be** beryllium 9.0122											5 **B** boron 10.811	6 **C** carbon 12.011	7 **N** nitrogen 14.007	8 **O** oxygen 15.999	9 **F** fluorine 18.998	10 **Ne** neon 20.180
11 **Na** sodium 22.990	12 **Mg** magnesium 24.305											13 **Al** aluminum 26.982	14 **Si** silicon 28.086	15 **P** phosphorus 30.974	16 **S** sulfur 32.065	17 **Cl** chlorine 35.453	18 **Ar** argon 39.948
19 **K** potassium 39.098	20 **Ca** calcium 40.078	21 **Sc** scandium 44.956	22 **Ti** titanium 47.867	23 **V** vanadium 50.942	24 **Cr** chromium 51.996	25 **Mn** manganese 54.938	26 **Fe** iron 55.845	27 **Co** cobalt 58.933	28 **Ni** nickel 58.693	29 **Cu** copper 63.546	30 **Zn** zinc 65.38	31 **Ga** gallium 69.723	32 **Ge** germanium 72.64	33 **As** arsenic 74.922	34 **Se** selenium 78.96	35 **Br** bromine 79.904	36 **Kr** krypton 83.798
37 **Rb** rubidium 85.468	38 **Sr** strontium 87.62	39 **Y** yttrium 88.906	40 **Zr** zirconium 91.224	41 **Nb** niobium 92.906	42 **Mo** molybdenum 95.96	43 **Tc** technetium [98]	44 **Ru** ruthenium 101.07	45 **Rh** rhodium 102.91	46 **Pd** palladium 106.42	47 **Ag** silver 107.87	48 **Cd** cadmium 112.41	49 **In** indium 114.82	50 **Sn** tin 118.71	51 **Sb** antimony 121.76	52 **Te** tellurium 127.60	53 **I** iodine 126.90	54 **Xe** xenon 131.29
55 **Cs** caesium 132.91	56 **Ba** barium 137.33	57–71	72 **Hf** hafnium 178.49	73 **Ta** tantalum 180.95	74 **W** tungsten 183.84	75 **Re** rhenium 186.21	76 **Os** osmium 190.23	77 **Ir** iridium 192.22	78 **Pt** platinum 195.08	79 **Au** gold 196.97	80 **Hg** mercury 200.59	81 **Tl** thallium 204.38	82 **Pb** lead 207.2	83 **Bi** bismuth 208.98	84 **Po** polonium [209]	85 **At** astatine [210]	86 **Rn** radon [222]
87 **Fr** francium [223]	88 **Ra** radium [226]	89–103	104 **Rf** rutherfordium [261]	105 **Db** dubnium [262]	106 **Sg** seaborgium [266]	107 **Bh** bohrium [264]	108 **Hs** hassium [277]	109 **Mt** meitnerium [268]	110 **Ds** darmstadtium [271]	111 **Rg** roentgenium [272]	112 **Cn** copernicium [277]	113 **Nh** nihonium [286]	114 **Fl** flerovium [289]	115 **Mc** moscovium [288]	116 **Lv** livermorium [298]	117 **Ts** tennessine [294]	118 **Og** oganesson [294]

57 **La** lanthanum 138.91	58 **Ce** cerium 140.12	59 **Pr** praseodymium 140.91	60 **Nd** neodymium 144.24	61 **Pm** promethium [145]	62 **Sm** samarium 150.36	63 **Eu** europium 151.96	64 **Gd** gadolinium 157.25	65 **Tb** terbium 158.93	66 **Dy** dysprosium 162.50	67 **Ho** holmium 164.93	68 **Er** erbium 167.26	69 **Tm** thulium 168.93	70 **Yb** ytterbium 173.05	71 **Lu** lutetium 174.97
89 **Ac** actinium [227]	90 **Th** thorium 232.04	91 **Pa** protactinium 231.04	92 **U** uranium 238.03	93 **Np** neptunium [237]	94 **Pu** plutonium [244]	95 **Am** americium [243]	96 **Cm** curium [247]	97 **Bk** berkelium [247]	98 **Cf** californium [251]	99 **Es** einsteinium [252]	100 **Fm** fermium [257]	101 **Md** mendelevium [258]	102 **No** nobelium [259]	103 **Lr** lawrencium [262]

There are many other elements. The elements combine in different ways to form the different molecules that make up all the matter we know. There are more than 100 elements in the periodic table. Scientists keep finding more.

In this book, you'll investigate the parts of an atom, how they behave, and how they come together to make different molecules. You'll also take a look at how substances change, what happens when two or more substances combine, and how chemistry plays a role in our world. Are you ready to learn about atoms and molecules? Let's go!

WORDS TO KNOW

chemistry: the science of how atoms and molecules combine to form substances and how those substances interact, combine, and change.

7

GOOD SCIENCE PRACTICES

Every good scientist keeps a science journal! As you read through this book and do the activities, keep track of your observations in a scientific method worksheet, like the one shown here. Scientists use the scientific method to keep their experiments organized.

Step	Example
1. Question: What are we trying to find out? What problem are we trying to solve?	Does a soccer ball weigh less than a bowling ball?
2. Research: What information is already known?	Books at the library say soccer balls weigh less than bowling balls.
3. Hypothesis/Prediction: What do we think the answer will be?	I think a soccer ball will weigh less than a bowling ball.
4. Equipment: What supplies are we using?	Soccer ball, bowling ball, science journal, scale
5. Method: What procedure are we following?	Use a scale to compare the weight of the soccer ball and bowling ball three times.
6. Results: What happened and why?	Which ball weighs more? Record your results!

Each chapter of this book begins with a question to help guide your exploration of atoms and molecules. Keep the question in your mind as you read the chapter. At the end of each chapter, use your science journal to record your thoughts and answers.

?

INVESTIGATE!

If everything is made of atoms, why do things look and feel different from each other?

PROJECT!

POINT A MASTERPIECE

Does pointillism really work? Create your own pointy artwork to find out.

1 Find a coloring page you want to color or outline artwork of your own.

2 Pick your art **medium**.

3 Fill in your coloring page using dots of color. Use two or more colors in one area to create a blended effect.

4 Try different media. Experiment with dots of different sizes. Are the results what you expected? What happens if you try making a picture this way without outlines?

THINK ABOUT IT: The dots in pointillism art are like molecules. They are individual pieces packed tightly together. From afar, they seem to be a solid mass. Can you think of other examples in which this is the case?

WORDS to KNOW

medium: the material artists use to create their art, such as crayons, paint, and ink. Plural is media.

PROJECT!
PIECING IT TOGETHER

A tangram is a square puzzle made from seven polygons, or tans. The tans can be put together to make many shapes. How many shapes can you make?

Here is a great website with tangram patterns for creating the tans and to see what shapes you can make.

SUPPLIES

* science journal and pencil
* tangram puzzle pattern
* heavy paper such as card stock

1 Print the tangram pattern and color the tans. Cut each piece out.

KEYWORD PROMPTS

ClipArt ETC Tangrams 🔍

2 Form the tans into different shapes. Follow the tangram rules.

* All seven tans must be used.
* All tans must lie flat.
* Each tan must touch at least one other tan.
* Tans must not overlap.
* Tans may be flipped and/or rotated.

3 Record your shapes in your notebook.

THINK ABOUT IT: The tans in a tangram are like atoms. There are a fixed number of them. They can be put together in different ways to make different things. However, there are limits to how they can be combined.

WORDS TO KNOW

polygon: a closed shape, made with all straight lines.

tan: one of the seven polygons that makes up a tangram.

PROJECT!

IS AIR REALLY MATTER?

SUPPLIES

* ✳ string or yarn
* ✳ science journal and pencil
* ✳ ruler, dowel, or other thin piece of wood
* ✳ 2 identical balloons

If you can't see something or hold it in your hand, is it matter? In this project, we'll test air to find out.

1 Start a scientific method worksheet in your science journal.

2 Cut a piece of string or yarn. Tie it to the middle of the ruler. Hold the top of the string. Does the ruler hang level? If not, adjust the string until the ruler hangs straight across.

3 Cut two equal pieces of string. Tie a string to the neck of each of the balloons. Tie one balloon on each end of the ruler. Make sure both strings are tied the same distance from the end of the ruler.

4 Hold the center string. Does the ruler still hang level?

5 Remove one of the balloons. Fill the balloon with air and knot it. Tie the balloon back into place.

6 Hold the center string. Look at the ruler. Does one side hang lower than the other? What does this prove?

THINK ABOUT IT: Matter is something that takes up space and has mass. Did you show that air is matter in your experiment? Are there other explanations for the results of your experiment?

CHAPTER 1

ATOMIC ARRANGEMENT

If you could see into an atom, you would see that it's not solid. There's a large core surrounded by smaller particles. Have you ever seen flies circling a pile of trash? This is similar to the inside of an atom!

The core of an atom is called the nucleus. This is the atom's heaviest part. The nucleus is packed with even smaller particles called neutrons and protons.

? INVESTIGATE!

What are the parts of an atom? Where are they found in the atom?

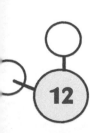

THE HEART OF IT

Neutrons and protons are about the same size. They have about the same mass. An atom has about the same numbers of protons and neutrons. Protons have a positive charge.

Neutrons have no charge. Charge is very important for keeping the atom together. We'll learn more about charge later in the chapter.

core: the middle part of something.

nucleus: the core of an atom.

neutron: a particle in the nucleus of an atom that has no charge.

proton: a particle in the nucleus of an atom that has a positive charge.

charge: a force of electricity that can be either positive or negative.

WORDS TO KNOW

An atom's protons tell what type of element the atom is. Remember, an element is a substance that is made of all the same kind of atoms. The number of protons is different for each element.

An element's atoms always have the same number of protons. This is not true for the neutrons. An element's atoms can have different numbers of neutrons.

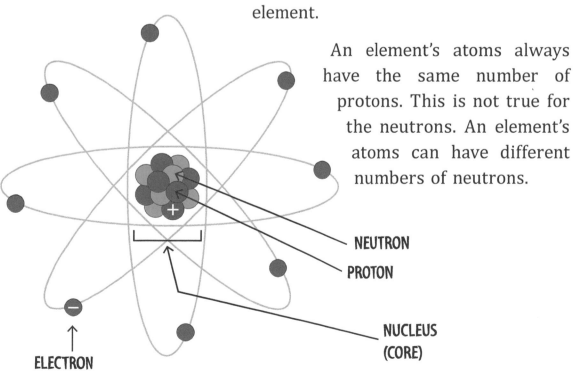

NEUTRON

PROTON

NUCLEUS
(CORE)

ELECTRON

electron: a particle in an atom with a negative charge that moves around the nucleus.

shell: the distance at which an electron moves around the nucleus.

atomic: about or relating to atoms.

atomic number: the number of protons in an atom's nucleus.

WORDS TO KNOW

SHELL GAME

Every atom contains a third type of particle. Electrons are very light. They travel around the nucleus in a path, always staying the same distance away. This path around the nucleus is called a shell.

Shells are also called energy levels. Atoms can have more than one shell. Each shell can have a certain number of electrons.

When a shell has all of the electrons it can hold, we say it's full. If the shell doesn't have all the electrons it can hold, it's not full. Electrons fill the atom's shells in order—the inner shell gets full first, then the next shell, and so on.

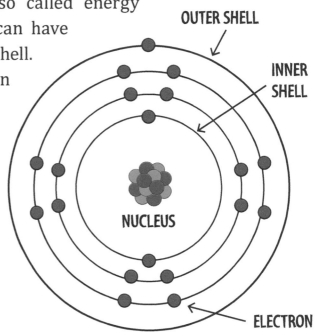

OUTER SHELL

INNER SHELL

NUCLEUS

ELECTRON

AR-YA-GON TO FIND THE ATOMIC NUMBER?

The number of protons is the element's **atomic number.** A hydrogen atom has one proton. An oxygen atom has eight. Look back to the periodic table on page 7. Find the hydrogen (H) and oxygen (O) elements. What are their atomic numbers? Find argon (Ar). What is argon's atomic number? How many protons does argon have?

CHARGE!

Have you ever played with magnets? One end of a magnet has a positive charge. The other end is negative. What happens when you put the positive ends, or poles, of two magnets together? What happens when you put the negative end near the positive end? Which way causes the magnets to be attracted to each other and which way causes them to repel?

Just like magnets, atoms have positive and negative charges. Electrons have a negative charge and protons have a positive charge. Because opposite charges attract, the positive protons pull the negative electrons close to the nucleus. This keeps the atom together.

The positive charge of the proton and the negative charge of the electron cancel each other out. This means that the atom is neutral. It has no charge. But sometimes, the atom changes a little bit and then it does have a charge!

attract: a force that pulls things closer, usually applied to a magnet.

repel: a force that pushes away.

strong force: the force between particles in an atom's nucleus.

neutral: having no charge.

WORDS TO KNOW

Did You Know?

A force called the strong force holds neutrons and protons together. The strong force is the strongest natural force there is. But it only works when the particles are almost touching. Can you think of other natural forces? What's holding you to the earth?

WORDS to KNOW

ion: an atom that has a positive or negative charge.

atomic weight: the average weight of an atom in an element.

compound: a substance made up of two or more elements.

An atom always has the same number of protons. Sometimes, an atom gains or loses an electron. If this happens, the atom becomes an ion. An ion is an atom with a charge. Extra electrons mean a negative charge. Missing electrons mean a positive charge.

STUDYING ATOMS

More than 2,000 year ago, ancient Greek scientists and thinkers believed atoms existed, but they had no proof. They didn't have the right instruments to study atoms. They thought atoms were tiny solids that couldn't be broken down. They thought atoms varied in size and shape and could combine to make different materials.

Skip ahead in time to 1800. English chemist John Dalton was studying gases. He came up with rules for atoms. He said that atoms were the tiny particles that made up elements. He thought all atoms in an element were exactly the same. He believed every atom had an atomic weight, which meant each element had a different atomic weight. Dalton also thought that atoms combined to create compounds.

Did You Know?

Scientists use models to learn more about what they're studying and to show other people their theories about science!

Many of Dalton's ideas were right. However, his vision of the atom was not. He imagined atoms like tiny balls. He thought compounds formed when the balls stuck together.

About 100 years after Dalton, physicist J.J. Thomson was studying electricity and magnets when he found a particle with a negative charge. This particle was 1,000 times smaller than the whole atom and about 1,800 times lighter. He had found the electron.

Thomson imagined an atom as a sea of positive charge in which thousands of negative particles floated. This model became known as the "plum pudding" model.

Five years later, scientists tested the plum pudding model. Hans Geiger and Ernest Marsden shot particles at gold foil. They expected the particles to pass straight through the foil. Many did, but some went off to the side and others bounced back completely.

HOW ATOMS ARE LIKE ONIONS

Have you ever peeled an onion? An onion is surrounded by layers of papery skin. You have to peel off layer after layer to get to the part you eat. Electron shells are a bit like onion skins. An atom with lots of electrons has many layers of electron shells surrounding its nucleus.

quark: a particle that makes up neutrons and protons.

WORDS TO KNOW

A physicist named Ernest Rutherford studied this experiment. In 1911, he proposed a new model. This one had lots of empty space. The protons all sat in the center as the nucleus. The electrons formed a cloud around the protons. The particles in the experiment passed through the empty space and bounced off the protons.

Niels Bohr improved this model a few years later. In his model, electrons have limited movement. They follow fixed paths. They also have different shells. The Bohr model looks a bit like planets orbiting the sun. In 1922, he earned a Nobel Prize in Physics for this model.

Did You Know?

There is also matter inside neutrons and protons. A quark is the most basic piece of matter. There are several different kinds of quarks. Up quarks and down quarks make up protons and neutrons. A proton has two up quarks and one down quark. A neutron has two down quarks and one up quark.

Scientists are still learning about what a real atom looks like. Today's atomic model is still based on what Rutherford and Bohr imagined more than 100 years ago.

Now that we know the parts of the atom, let's take a closer look at elements!

? CONSIDER AND DISCUSS

It's time to consider and discuss: What are the parts of an atom? Where are they found in the atom?

PROJECT!
PLATE SOME HELIUM

You've seen helium balloon floating around at parties. What does a helium atom look like? You can make a simple model of a helium atom using a paper plate.

SUPPLIES

* ✳ science journal and pencil
* ✳ 4 bottle caps
* ✳ permanent marker
* ✳ 12 pony beads (6 each of 2 different colors)
* ✳ 2 small beads, same color
* ✳ paper plate
* ✳ glue

1 Color the bottle caps to be two different colors. Pick one color for the neutrons and one for the protons.

2 Pick one color pony bead for the up quarks and one for the down quarks.

3 Fill the bottle caps with glue. Put two up quarks and one down quark in each proton. Put two down quarks and one up quark in each neutron.

4 Glue the protons and neutrons to the center of the plate to create the nucleus. Glue the electrons (the remaining two beads) around the edge of the plate.

THINK ABOUT IT: Think about what you know about the size and mass of the parts of an atom. What would you need to change to make this model more accurate?

WHAT DID THE VENDER SAY WHEN A NEUTRON ASKED, "HOW MUCH FOR A HOT DOG?"

"For you, no charge!"

19

PROJECT!

SPINNING OXYGEN

When scientists make a model, it often stands still because of the materials it's made from. But real atoms never stop moving! Here, you'll create an oxygen model that spins.

SUPPLIES

* ✳ science journal and pencil
* ✳ 3 paper plates or pieces of cardboard or card stock
* ✳ markers, crayons, or small paper circles in 3 different colors
* ✳ 1 metal brad

1 Cut two of the paper plates into smaller circles, one larger than the other, so you have three circles that are large, medium, and small.

2 Prick a hole in the center of each circle with a pin or push-pin.

3 Stack the circles. Put the largest on the bottom, the medium circle in the middle, and the smallest circle on top. Line the circles up at their centers. Fasten the circles together using the metal brad. The circles should stay together, but they should be able to spin independently. The small circle is your nucleus and the other two circles are your two electron shells.

4 Choose colors for the elements in your atom. What color are the electrons, protons, and neutrons?

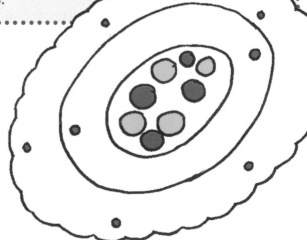

5 Add eight protons and eight neutrons to the nucleus.

6 Add electrons to their shells. There are eight total electrons. Two go in the first energy level. How many go in the outer shell?

THINK ABOUT IT: How is this model different from an actual oxygen atom? How correct is the movement of electrons?

Did You Know?

If an atom was the size of a football stadium, the nucleus would be about the size of a marble.

THREE WAYS TO DRAW A CIRCLE

* Use a math compass. This is a tool that looks like an upside-down "V." There is a point on one side and a pencil on the other. You can set the compass to the size circle you want to draw.

* Find objects that have the size circle you want, such as a cup, a bowl, or a can. Trace around the edge of the object.

* Use printed circles. Many paper plates already have circles on them. Use them as your guide.

MAGNET MAGIC

SUPPLIES

* science journal and pencil
* string or yarn
* scissors
* clean, dry plastic bottle
* paper clip
* strong magnet

Electrons are drawn to an atom's nucleus like metal objects are drawn to magnets. In this activity, you can explore the science of magnetism.

1 Cut the yarn to about one and a half times the length of the bottle.

2 Tie the paper clip to one end of the yarn. Trim off the excess yarn so that it doesn't touch the bottle in the next step.

3 Place the paper clip in the bottle. Let down the yarn until the paper clip just touches the bottom of the bottle. Screw the lid on the bottle. The paper clip should be hanging in the air inside the bottle.

4 Set the bottle on a solid surface. Wait until the paper clip is still. Touch the magnet to the side of the bottle near the paper clip. What happens? Try different areas on the bottle. What do you notice?

TRY THIS: What happens if you use a larger bottle? What if the bottle is made of glass? Try different magnets. How do these changes affect your results?

CHAPTER 2

IT'S ELEMENT-ARY!

There are more than 100 elements, and scientists keep finding more! Elements make up everything we know, including our own bodies and our planet. Most of them form in nature, but some are elements that people have created. How do scientists keep track of them all?

The periodic table is a bit like a dictionary of elements. Every element has its own entry on the table. You can look at its entry and learn a lot about that element.

? INVESTIGATE!

Why is it important to keep information about the elements organized in a chart?

WHAT'S IN AN ELEMENT'S ENTRY?

Each element has an official name and symbol. The symbol is an abbreviation of the name. The element named carbon has a symbol of C.

There are also numbers in every entry that give information about the element. The top number is the atomic number. Remember, this is the number of protons the element has. Carbon has an atomic number of six. How many protons does it have?

ATOMIC NUMBER

6

C

← **ABBREVIATION**

Carbon ← **NAME**
12.011

ATOMIC WEIGHT

The numbers of electrons and protons inside an atom must match so that the atom has no charge. If a carbon atom has six protons, how many electrons must it have?

Each entry on the periodic table gives us lots of information about the atoms in an element, just as a dictionary gives lots of information about each word!

SILLY SYMBOLS

It makes sense that the element carbon has a symbol of C and hydrogen has a symbol of H. But why does gold have the symbol Au? Why is lead Pb? These letters are abbreviations of the Latin forms of the element names. In Latin, silver is *argentum* and lead is *plumbum*. Look through the periodic table. How many of the symbols are different from what you would expect?

READING THE PERIODIC TABLE

Scientists use the periodic table to organize the known elements in a way that makes sense.

The periodic table has 18 columns and seven rows. Columns go up and down, while rows go across. It might look like there are nine rows, but those last two at the bottom actually fit into column three, rows six and seven.

You can read the periodic table as though you were reading a book. Moving from left to right, the elements increase in atomic number. Hydrogen, with the lowest atomic number, is at the upper left. Oganesson, with the highest atomic number, is at the lower right. The elements at the top tend to be lightest. The ones at the bottom are heaviest.

The elements fall into two main families—metals and nonmetals. A metal conducts heat. When you boil water, what is the pot or kettle made of? Usually, it's made of metal. Heat travels easily through metal. Metals also conduct electricity.

metal: an element that is a hard, shiny material. It conducts heat and electricity and can be melted.

nonmetal: an element that does not have the properties of a metal.

conduct: to act as the channel through which something travels.

WORDS TO KNOW

Most metals are solid at room temperature. They are usually shiny. They can often be bent into different shapes. Nonmetal elements don't have these properties. Nonmetals can be gases or solids. It's not easy to change the shape of solid nonmetals.

Some elements are tricky. Metalloids act like metals, but sometimes they act like nonmetals. Sometimes, they conduct electricity, but not always!

Each row of the periodic table is a called a period. Elements in a period have the same number of electron shells, or energy levels. Row one has one shell. Row two has two shells. How many shells do you think row four has? Row seven?

Each column is called a group. Elements in a group all have the same number of valence electrons. These are the electrons in an atom's outermost shell. Group one is the first column. All elements in this column have one electron in their outer shell.

Did You Know?

The element silicon is the base material for most computers. Do you use a smartphone or tablet? It probably has silicon inside of it!

The last group contains a type of element called noble gases. All of these elements have full outer shells.

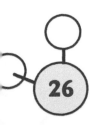

All of these elements have eight electrons in their outer shells, except helium, which only has two. It is still considered a noble gas because the first shell can hold only two electrons.

electrical current: the flow of electrons through a material.

conductor: a material through which electricity and heat move easily.

insulator: a material that prevents heat, sound, or electricity from passing through it easily.

WORDS TO KNOW

IT'S ELECTRIC!

Have you seen electrical wires? They are strung between poles on the side of the road. They also run from an outlet to a lamp. You probably know these wires carry electricity. But what exactly is electricity?

Electricity is the flow of electrons. They don't gush like water in a waterfall. It's more like dominoes falling. An electron from one atom bumps over to the next atom. This bumps an electron out of that atom and into the next one. This happens again and again to make **electrical current**.

A **conductor** is a material through which electricity flows easily. This is made possible by loose electrons. The outer electrons must be free to move. **Insulators** are materials whose electrons are tightly bound. Electrons can't flow through insulators. Most metals are conductors. Most nonmetals are insulators. Some materials, such as carbon, can be both. It all depends on how the atoms are put together.

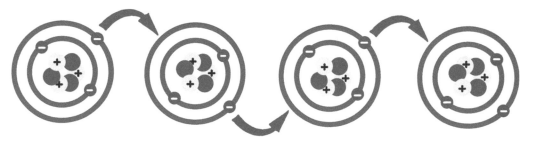

CREATING THE PERIODIC TABLE

For hundreds of years, scientists tried to find a good way to organize the elements into a table that everyone could read and understand.

An scientist named Dmitri Mendeleev (1834–1907) had the most success. In 1869, Mendeleev made a card for each of the 62 known elements. On each card, he wrote the element's properties. He then played scientist solitaire, ordering and reordering the cards over and over.

Finally, Mendeleev came up with a good order. He placed the elements in increasing atomic weight. However, he felt that some of the elements weren't in the right place. He thought there were missing elements and wondered if some atomic weights were wrong.

The periodic table used today is based on his work. The missing elements are there now. The table is no longer based on atomic weight—instead, the elements increase by atomic number.

MENDELEEV'S PERIODIC TABLE

Mendeleev first published a periodic table in 1869. He used question marks to note missing elements and elements whose atomic weights he thought were wrong. How do they differ from today's periodic table? How are they the same? Why was it important that Mendeleev left room for yet-to-be-discovered elements?

PS You can see some of his early notes as well as his first published table at this website.

KEYWORD PROMPTS

AIP periodic table

ID, PLEASE

Imagine you are a scientist holding a hunk of an element for the first time. How do you know what you have? The best way is to compare its properties to those of elements you know.

Start with the state of the element at room temperature. If it's liquid, your job is easy—it has to be one of two things. Only bromine and mercury are liquid at room temperature.

Solids and gases aren't as simple. There are lots of them! Many are similar in color. Scientists use other properties to identify gases and solids.

melting point: the temperature at which a solid melts.

boiling point: the temperature at which a liquid boils.

ductile: describes something that can be hammered thin or drawn out into a wire without breaking.

brittle: describes something that can be easily broken or snapped.

WORDS TO KNOW

Did You Know?

Element 101 is mendelevium, named after Dmitri Mendeleev. Scientists discovered it in 1955. Mendelevium is a manmade metal that does not have any uses yet. In fact, only a few atoms of mendelevium have even been made.

Other properties include the melting point and boiling point. When a solid is heated, at some point it melts and turns into a liquid. The temperature at which a liquid begins to boil is the boiling point.

Does the material change when it's exposed to air or water? The speed with which it reacts is called its reactivity. Can it be pulled into wires or pounded into thick sheets? Does it snap when you try to bend it? An element that bends easily is called ductile, while a brittle element snaps.

There are many other ways to describe the properties of a material. Each property gives a hint as to what a material is.

Now that we know about the most basic forms of matter, let's see what happens when these atoms start to combine to form other substances!

 CONSIDER AND DISCUSS

It's time to consider and discuss: Why is it important to keep information about the elements organized in a chart?

PROJECT!

DESCRIBE IT!

SUPPLIES

* science journal and pencil
* objects for observation

Scientists rely on descriptions. They record what they see. They keep track of changes. This helps them identify materials and give information to other scientists. Practice your observation skills in this activity.

Caution: Never sniff a powdery or liquid substance too hard—you could hurt your nose and eyes!

1 Pick an object to observe. It could be a toy, such as Legos or marbles. Perhaps it's something you eat or drink, such as cereal, rice, or juice. Maybe it's something that makes up part of your house, such as the counter or floor.

2 Observe your object by looking at, feeling, smelling, and listening to it.

3 Write a description of the object in your science journal. Try to find several things to describe about the object. Use specific words. Don't say, "It smells bad." Instead, think of other things it smells like or looks like. Does it smell like rotting fish or dog poop?

WHAT TOOL CAN YOU MAKE FROM POTASSIUM, NICKEL, AND IRON?

A KNiFe.

TRY THIS! Write your description on an index card. Give it to someone else. Can they figure out what you're describing?

PROJECT!
COLOR CODE THE PERIODIC TABLE

Periodic tables are often colorful. The colors point out important information. Explore and color your own.

SUPPLIES

* periodic table printout
* colored pencils, crayons, or markers

1 Print out a black-and-white periodic table. See page 35 for ideas on where to find one.

2 Pick colors for the following groups: liquid, gas, metal, noble gases, magnetic metals, noble metals, manmade, and **radioactive**. Make a color key. Note which color matches each label.

3 Draw a circle around the symbols for each element that is a gas at room temperature. These elements are H, He, N, O, F, Ne, Cl, Ar, Kr, Xe, Rn, and Og.

4 Draw a triangle around the symbols for each element that is a liquid at room temperature. These are Br and Hg.

5 Draw a box around each element in the column of noble gases.

6 Outline the metals. This is a jagged line that includes Al, Ge, Sb, Po, Ts, and all elements to the left and below.

7 Outline the magnetic metals. These include elements 26–28.

WORDS TO KNOW

radioactive: describes an atom whose nucleus can break down, forming a different kind of atom.

chemical: another word for a substance.

8 Outline the noble metals. These include elements 44–47 and 75–79.

9 Color the manmade elements. These are not found in nature and include elements 95–118.

10 Draw a box around the symbols for the radioactive elements. These are elements 43, 61, and 84–118.

TRY THIS! Print out another copy of the periodic table. Color in the elements that make up the human body.

FULL OF CHEMICALS

You might see a product at the grocery store marked, "chemical free," but actually, chemical elements make up everything in the world! There are more than 25 of them in the human body. We are made mostly of 11 different elements, and the rest are trace elements. This means they are there in tiny quantities.

ELEMENTS IN THE HUMAN BODY BY PERCENT WEIGHT

* Oxygen 65%
* Carbon 18%
* Hydrogen 9.5%
* Nitrogen 3.2%
* Calcium 1.5%
* Phosphorus 1%

* Potassium 0.4%
* Sodium 0.2%
* Chlorine 0.2%
* Magnesium 0.1%
* Sulfur 0.04%
* Trace elements 0.86%

PROJECT!
ELEMENT CATCHER

Each element is unique. Pick an element that seems interesting to you and research it. Create an element catcher to share some facts about your element.

SUPPLIES

* element catcher printout
* Internet access or book of elements
* pencil
* scissors
* colored pencils, crayons, or markers

1 On each of the outside corners of your element catcher, write one of the following.

- The element's name
- The element's symbol
- The element's number
- Whether the element is metal or nonmetal

2 Provide element information in the triangle below each prompt.

- What date was the element discovered?
- Who discovered it?
- Describe the element at room temperature. Include its color.
- Where is the element used?
- How many protons are in an atom of your element?
- Where can you find it?
- At what temperature does it melt?
- Include a fun fact about the element.

3 Color your catcher and add pictures. Cut out the catcher.

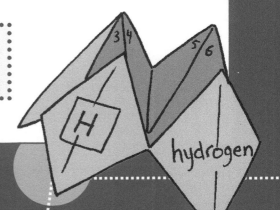

PROJECT!

4 Fold in half on the diagonal by folding one corner over to meet the opposite corner so the paper makes a triangle. Unfold.

5 Repeat step 4 for the other diagonal. You now have creases that make an X on the paper.

6 Place the catcher with the writing facing down. Fold each corner in to meet the center point. Turn the catcher over. Fold each corner in to meet the center point.

7 Fold in half. Slide your fingers into the flaps of the catcher. Move your fingers so the catcher opens up. Move your fingers apart to open one way. Close them. Keep fingers together and move hands apart. This opens it the other way.

8 Show your catcher to a friend. Ask them to make a selection. Alternate between opening the catcher up and apart. Spell out their choice or count the element number. Stop with the catcher open.

9 Have your friend choose a number from those shown. Alternate between opening the catcher up and apart. Count to the chosen number. Stop with the catcher open. Have your friend select a topic. Open the topic flap and read the selection.

Did You Know?

You can find periodic tables on the Internet with an adult's permission. Here are a few.

KEYWORD PROMPTS

Los Alamos National Laboratory 🔍

Jefferson Laboratory

Royal Society of Chemistry

PROJECT!
ELEMENTAL SUPERHERO

SUPPLIES

* Internet access or book of elements
* science journal and pencil
* colored pencils, crayons, or markers

Each element is amazing in its own way. Some have inspired comic book heroes. Have you ever heard of Iron Man? How about the Silver Surfer? Now is your chance to invent your own. Pick an element and use it to create a superhero.

Caution: Ask an adult for permission before you go on the Internet.

1 Pick an element to be the basis of your superhero.

- Where does your superhero come from?

- What is your superhero's special power? Do they have more than one?

- Is there something that can weaken or destroy your superhero? Think of Superman and kryptonite.

2 Come up with a name for your superhero and draw a picture. Use the color of the element somewhere. Is it the color of your hero's eyes, skin, costume, or something else?

TRY THIS! Make up a story with your new superhero as the main character.

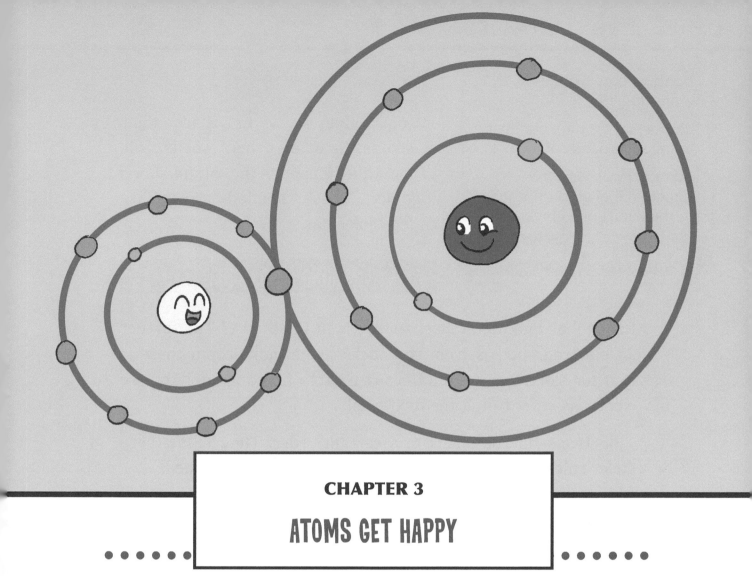

CHAPTER 3

ATOMS GET HAPPY

· ·

**What makes an atom happy? Full electron shells!
Just as humans are happy with full bellies, atoms are
happy when their electron shells are complete.**

● ●

Very few atoms have full electron shells. Those that do are in the noble gas family. Can you find the noble gases on the periodic table on page 7? All other atoms either have too many electrons or too few.

?

INVESTIGATE!

How do atoms join together to make new chemicals?

WORDS TO KNOW

bond: a force that holds atoms together.

clockwise: the direction that follows the hands of a clock.

counterclockwise: the direction that goes opposite to the hands of a clock.

Atoms give away or share their electrons to make their shells full. When this happens, the atoms bond together. These bonded atoms are called molecules.

MAKING A FULL SHELL

Remember looking at electron shells in Chapter 1? The further an electron shell is from the nucleus, the more room there is in it for electrons. A shell doesn't have to fill completely before electrons start filling the next shell.

Electrons fill the shells in a certain order. They follow very strict rules when they are placing themselves in the shells.

An atom is happiest when its valence shell has eight electrons in it. This might not be the maximum number of electrons that can fit in that shell. It is simply the number that makes the atom the most stable, or happiest.

ELECTRON SPIN

Electrons move within their shells. They don't move like planets circling the sun. They move in a random pattern that zigs and zags. While electrons move around their shells in this random way, they also spin. Some electrons spin clockwise, while others spin counterclockwise.

ionic bond: a chemical bond formed between ions of opposing charges.

OPPOSITES ATTRACT

Atoms are always trying to be happier. They really want those eight valence electrons! To get this, they do some bonding.

Sodium (Na) is element 11, which means it has 11 electrons. It has three shells. Shell one has two electrons. Shell two has eight. That leaves just one electron in shell three.

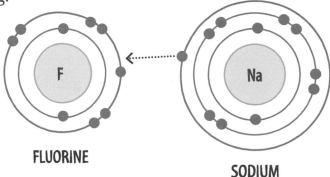

FLUORINE

SODIUM

Fluorine (F) is element 9, which means it has nine electrons. Fluorine has two shells, with two electrons in shell one and seven in shell two.

Sodium has one electron in its outer shell. Fluorine is missing one electron in its outer shell. They seem made for each other!

When a sodium atom meets a fluorine atom, it gives its extra electron. This makes both atoms ions. The sodium ion has a positive charge because it has one less electron than protons. The fluorine ion has a negative charge because it has one more electron than protons.

Since opposites attract, the negative ion, fluorine, is pulled toward the positive one, sodium to form an *ionic bond*. The result is sodium fluoride (NaF). This is an important ingredient of toothpaste!

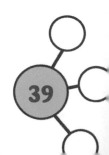

39

covalent bond: a chemical bond where atoms share electrons.

WORDS TO KNOW

SHARING ATOMS ARE HAPPY ATOMS

Not all atoms give electrons to other atoms. Sometimes, they simply share. This sharing of electrons is called a covalent bond.

Let's look at the element chlorine (Cl). Each atom has seven valence electrons. They each need just one more. Imagine there were two chlorine atoms. What if they each shared one of their electrons with the other?

If the chlorine atoms shared an electron, they would both have eight valence electrons. The bonding of two chlorine atoms with a covalent bond makes a chlorine gas molecule (Cl_2).

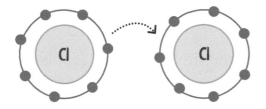

CHLORINE + CHLORINE = CHLORINE GAS (Cl_2)

Covalent bonds can also happen between atoms of different elements. They can even occur between more than two atoms. For example, carbon (C) has four valence electrons. It wants another four electrons to fill its outer shell.

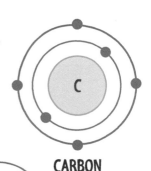

CARBON

A hydrogen (H) atom has one electron in the first shell. This shell holds two electrons. The atom wants to find another electron to fill its empty space.

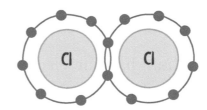

HYDROGEN

double bond: a covalent bond where two pairs of electrons are shared.

WORDS TO KNOW

When a carbon atom meets a bunch of hydrogen atoms, they bond. Four hydrogen atoms share their electrons with the carbon atom. This forms four covalent bonds, and all five atoms end up happy. The new molecule is methane (CH_4). Methane is a natural gas that is used to heat homes and cook food.

CARBON + HYDROGEN + HYDROGEN + HYDROGEN + HYDROGEN = METHANE (CH_4)

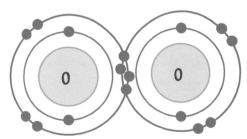

Atoms can share more than one electron. Let's take a look at oxygen (O). It has six valence electrons, and it wants eight to make a full shell. If two oxygen molecules get together, they can each share two electrons with the other. This makes an oxygen gas molecule. The atoms are connected by covalent bonds. Since each atom shares two electrons, this is called a *double bond.*

· Did You Know? · · · · ·

Methane is released when bodies decompose. Turkey vultures, which eat dead bodies, follow the smell of methane to find dinner.

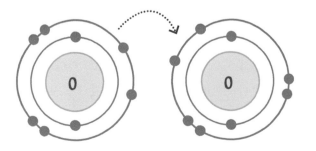

OXYGEN + OXYGEN = OXYGEN GAS (O_2)

SEEING DOTS

Atoms give and share electrons to create bonds between themselves. There are lots of electrons floating around. It can be hard to keep track of!

In 1916, a chemist named Gilbert N. Lewis (1875–1946) came up with a way to diagram the interactions between atoms. His diagrams are called Lewis dot structures, or Lewis dot diagrams.

Lewis dot diagrams show the element symbol, which stands for the atom, and dots around that symbol that stand for the valence electrons. For most elements, eight dots make a complete shell. For hydrogen and helium, two dots make a complete shell.

Look at the dot diagrams on the following page for the first elements on the periodic table. What do you notice about them? What do you notice about all the elements in each group, or column? Can you see how certain atoms will pair up with other atoms to share electrons? Remember, atoms are trying to get eight electrons in their outer shell. Which atoms will pair up with each other?

Number of valence electrons							
1	2	3	4	5	6	7	8
H.							He:
Li .	.Be.	. B .	. C .	: N .	: O .	: F .	:Ne:
Na.	.Mg.	.Al .	. Si .	: P .	: S .	: Cl .	: Ar :
K .	.Ca.	.Ga.	.Ge.	: As .	: Se .	: Br .	: Kr :
Rb.	. Sr .	. In .	. Sn .	: Sb .	: Te .	: I .	: Xe :

These diagrams can help us see how bonds form. Let's look at sodium and fluorine again. See how they combine using dot diagrams? The dot, or electron, from sodium is given to fluorine to complete its shell. Both atoms are bonded and happy.

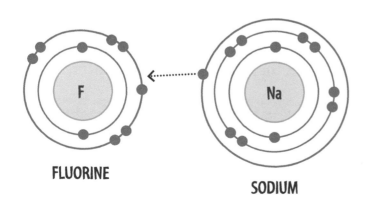

FLUORINE

SODIUM

$$Na \cdot + :\overset{..}{\underset{..}{F}} \cdot = [Na]^{+} \ [:\overset{..}{\underset{..}{F}}:]^{-}$$

43

CUBIC ATOMS

Gilbert N. Lewis was the first scientist to suggest that atoms bond through shared electrons. He thought the electrons in atoms were shaped like boxes. The boxes could be inside each other, but the atom wanted an electron at each corner of the outer box. How do you think this way of thinking about the atom led to the invention of the dot diagrams?

  You can see some of Lewis's cubic atoms at this website.

KEYWORD PROMPTS

Chemical Heritage Lewis

Dot diagrams also show covalent bonds. Here are diagrams for chlorine gas (Cl_2) and oxygen gas (O_2).

$$:\overset{..}{\underset{..}{Cl}}\cdot \ + \ \cdot\overset{..}{\underset{..}{Cl}}: \ = \ :\overset{..}{\underset{..}{Cl}}:\overset{..}{\underset{..}{Cl}}:$$

$$:\overset{.}{\underset{..}{O}}\cdot \ + \ \cdot\overset{.}{\underset{..}{O}}: \ = \ \overset{..}{\underset{..}{O}}::\overset{..}{\underset{..}{O}}$$

With Lewis dot diagrams, each pair of shared electrons can be replaced with a line. The oxygen atoms in O_2 share two sets of electrons. This is shown with a double line.

You've learned about the smallest parts of atoms and how atoms bond to make other types of molecules. In the next chapter, we'll see how molecules mix together to become even more kinds of matter!

 CONSIDER AND DISCUSS!

It's time to consider and discuss: How do atoms join together to make new chemicals?

PROJECT!

ELECTRON DANCE

Can you move like an electron? Try this activity alone or with friends to find out. If you want, add music and make it an electron dance!

SUPPLIES

✳ chair, large box, or other object to act as nucleus
✳ open floor space
✳ music (optional)

1 Place your nucleus in the middle of your open floor space.

2 Each person is an electron. How many people do you have? What atom would that be?

3 Have everyone take a starting position around the nucleus. Use what you know about shells.

4 Start moving around the nucleus as if you were an electron. Use what you know about how electrons move.

THINK ABOUT IT: What difficulties did you have in trying to move like an electron? In what ways do you think electrons move the same? In what ways do you think they're different?

MAKE ELECTRONS SPIN

In an earlier activity, you made an atom that could spin. Electrons spin, too. In this activity, we'll make another atomic model of helium. This time, we'll add spinning electrons.

SUPPLIES

* scissors
* paper or card stock
* pencil
* 3 metal brads
* pin or needle
* colored pencils, crayons, or markers

1 Draw one large circle, about 3.5 inches wide, on a piece of card stock or paper. This will be the nucleus.

2 Draw two small circles. Each should be about 1 inch wide. These will be the electrons.

3 Draw two thin rectangles. Each should be about a half inch by 5.5 inches. These will connect the electrons to the nucleus.

4 Mark the center of each circle with a dot. Mark the center of each end of the rectangles with a dot. These dots should be about a half inch from each end.

5 Cut out the shapes. Use the pin to poke a hole where the dots are.

6 Pair each electron with a rectangle. Connect each electron to its rectangle using a metal brad. Push the brad through the pin holes.

PROJECT!

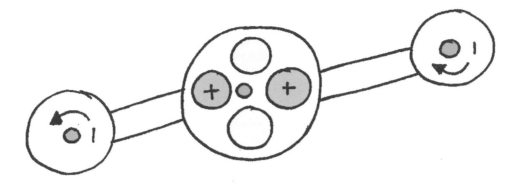

7 Arrange the rectangles so the electrons are facing up. Place the other end of the rectangles behind the nucleus. Connect the nucleus to the rectangles using a brad. Push the brad through the nucleus first. Then push it through both rectangles and open the clasp.

8 Draw an arrow on each electron to indicate its spin. One should spin clockwise. The other should spin counterclockwise.

TRY THIS: Draw and color protons and neutrons in the nucleus. What are the electrical charges of each particle?

WHAT DID THE MOLECULE SAY IN THE MORNING?

Time to get up and atom!

PROJECT!
PUZZLING ATOMS

Atoms fit together in different ways. Let's see how many ways we can put a few together.

1 Draw the shapes in the picture on paper or cardboard.

2 Color each atom a different color. Use a color related to the element. For example, you could make chlorine light blue because it reminds you of swimming pools.

3 Glue the shapes to card stock. Be sure the glue covers the edges of each of the atoms. Cut out each of the atoms.

4 Fit the atoms together to make molecules. Record your molecules in your science journal.

THINK ABOUT IT: What kind of bonds do you think these atoms form?

SUPPLIES

* science journal and pencil
* scissors
* colored pencils, crayons, or markers
* card stock or light cardboard (cereal boxes work well)
* glue stick

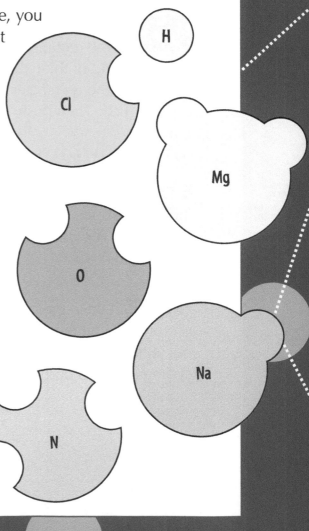

PROJECT!

MARSH-MOLECULES

Oxygen molecules share electrons. You can model this with marshmallows!

SUPPLIES

* ☀ science journal and pencil
* ☀ 2 large marshmallows
* ☀ 14 mini marshmallows
* ☀ 16 toothpicks

1 Place eight toothpicks in each of two large marshmallows. Each large marshmallow represents a nucleus.

2 For each large marshmallow, place six mini marshmallows on six of the toothpicks.

3 Move two toothpicks and mini marshmallows. Four mini marshmallows should be shared between the two large marshmallows.

4 Document your molecule in your science journal. Find the oxygen atom on the dot diagram. How many valence electrons does it have?

TRY THIS! Make a marshmallow model for other molecules. Can you make H_2 and N_2? Here is an example of Cl_2.

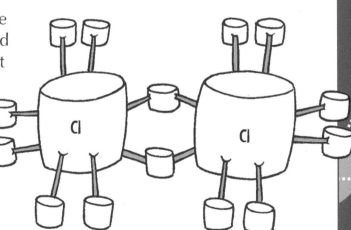

CHLORINE GAS (Cl_2)

CHAPTER 4

MIX IT UP!

Atoms can bond to each other in seemingly infinite ways. When different atoms bond together, they form all the materials that make up our world.

You learned in the last chapter that atoms bond together to form molecules. When all the atoms bonded together are the same, the substance they make is an element. A molecule made from at least two different types of atoms is a compound. Some compounds contain lots of different kinds of atoms!

INVESTIGATE!

What is the difference between a mixture and a solution? How can you tell them apart?

infinite: with no limit, going on forever.

WORDS TO KNOW

Compounds don't act like the elements that make them. For example, pure sodium (Na) is a soft, shiny metal. If you put it in water, it reacts. Sometimes, it will even burst into flame!

Chlorine (Cl) is a greenish-yellow gas that is poisonous. People use solid chlorine in swimming pools to kill germs, but if you breathe in the gas, it can kill you. Sodium bonds with chlorine to form sodium chloride (NaCl). You probably have sodium chloride in your kitchen—it's the salt you might put on your food! These two dangerous elements combine to make something we eat.

WHAT'S IN A NAME?

Every chemical has both a formula and a name. These tell us what elements are in the chemical. Formulas use element symbols. Names use the element names, with a few changes.

chemical reaction: the action that occurs between atoms or molecules to form one or more new substances.

WORDS ⊕ KNOW

Earlier in the book we talked about the chemical O_2. This is oxygen gas. The formula O_2 tells what is in an oxygen molecule. The letter O stands for the oxygen atom, and the small 2 tells us that there are two atoms in the molecule.

A water molecule has the formula H_2O. The letter H is the hydrogen symbol, the O is oxygen, and the small 2 means that there are two hydrogen atoms for every one oxygen atom.

Did You Know?

Have you heard of a chemical called dihydrogen monoxide? This chemical is actually water!

The names of compounds are usually combinations of the element names. Some compounds are known only by a common name. Water (H_2O) is one of these. Ammonia (NH_3) is another. Other compounds have names that tell us how to make one of its molecules.

THE MAKING OF A (GIANT) MOLECULE

In 2011, Swiss scientists created a beast. It was a giant molecule with a small name. It took 170,000 **chemical reactions** to make PG5. A diagram of PG5 looked like a bushy tree. It weighed the same as 200 million hydrogen atoms. This was the largest molecule ever made by people. In the future, it could be used to deliver medicine to a certain part of the body. **You can see a picture of PG5 at this website.**

KEYWORD PROMPTS

PG5 image 🔍

COMPOUND VS. MIXTURE

A compound contains a mix of atoms. But this does not make it a mixture! What is the difference between mixtures and compounds?

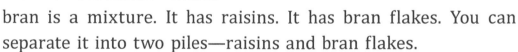

mixture: a mix of two or more substances that are not chemically bonded together.

ratio: the relationship in size or quantity between two things.

WORDS TO KNOW

Compounds form when atoms bond together. Once this happens, the atoms aren't easy to tear apart. There is only one way to break a compound into its parts. You need to break its bonds. This destroys the compound.

When materials mix together to form mixtures, these materials do not bond together. The materials are not chemically connected. They can be separated without destroying anything.

Do you ever eat raisin bran for breakfast? Raisin bran is a mixture. It has raisins. It has bran flakes. You can separate it into two piles—raisins and bran flakes.

Compounds always have the same ratio of parts. For example, each molecule of water (H_2O) contains one oxygen atom and two hydrogen atoms. Water is always 88.8 percent oxygen and 11.2 percent hydrogen, by weight. If you pour a glass of water, it will be 88.8 percent oxygen and 11.2 percent hydrogen. If you drink half of it, the remaining water is still 88.8 percent oxygen and 11.2 percent hydrogen.

homogeneous mixture: a mixture where all particles are evenly distributed.

heterogeneous mixture: a mixture where particles are not evenly spread out.

WORDS TO KNOW

Mixtures, however, are not exact. A bowl of jelly beans is a mixture. It has a variety of colors and flavors. A bowl of jelly beans might have red, green, yellow, purple, and orange in equal amounts. If you eat some red ones and your friend eats all the purple, the ratio in your bowl is different. You have fewer red and purple jelly beans compared to the rest, but it's still a mixture of jelly beans.

DIFFERENT KINDS OF MIXTURES

Mixtures can be put together in different ways. Some have their parts spread very evenly throughout the mixture. This is a homogeneous mixture. The mixture has the same makeup all the way through. A cloudless sky is an example of a homogenous mixture. Air is a mixture of different gases mixed evenly together.

Other mixtures might have clumps or patches spread out unevenly. Remember the bowl of raisin bran cereal? There are lots of flakes. There are clumps of raisins on top of the flakes. Many single raisins sink to the

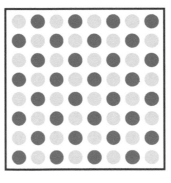

HOMOGENEOUS

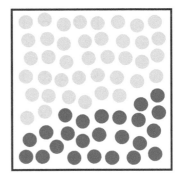

HETEROGENEOUS

bottom of the bowl. The raisins aren't evenly spaced in the cereal. This is a heterogeneous mixture. The parts are spread unevenly through the mixture.

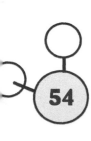

Sand is another heterogeneous mixture. It has different colored grains in it that aren't spread evenly. It doesn't look the same everywhere.

A solution is a homogeneous mixture of tiny particles the size of atoms or molecules. When you add salt to water, it dissolves. Salt water is a solution. The salt and the water are mixed very evenly. If you were to drink it, would some parts taste fresh and others taste salty? No, the whole drink would be salty. Yuck!

solution: the result when one substance has dissolved into another.

dissolve: to mix with a liquid and become part of the liquid.

solute: a substance that dissolves into another to make a solution.

solvent: a substance that can dissolve other substances.

WORDS TO KNOW

The parts of a solution have names, too. In salt water, salt is a solute. It is the thing being dissolved. Water is a solvent. The solvent does the dissolving. In solutions, a small amount of solute mixes with a larger amount of solvent to make a solution.

Did You Know?

Air is 78 percent nitrogen and 21 percent oxygen. It has bits of lots of other things, too, including water vapor, argon (Ar), and carbon dioxide (CO_2). It can even have bacteria floating in it.

All of these mixtures and solutions make up the things in our world. But they take different forms at different times under different conditions. We'll learn about the ways in which matter changes in the next chapter.

CONSIDER AND DISCUSS

It's time to consider and discuss: What is the difference between a mixture and a solution? How can you tell them apart?

PROJECT!

FIND-IT MIX

SUPPLIES

* clear jar or bottle with lid
* assorted small objects
* unpopped corn kernels, rice, lentils, or other small items

Mixtures are everywhere! Pay attention at the dinner table and you're likely to discover several mixtures right on your plate. You can make your own mixture into a fun game with this activity.

1 Make sure your jar or bottle is clean and dry.

2 Collect an assortment of small objects that fit in the jar.

3 After placing the objects in the jar, pour the popcorn kernels on top. Fill the jar with the kernels. Place the lid on the jar and shake it to distribute the materials.

4 To play, challenge a friend to see how many hidden objects they can find without opening the jar. Shaking is allowed!

THINK ABOUT IT: What makes this a mixture? Is it homogeneous or heterogeneous? How can you separate the items when you are done playing the game?

PROJECT!

WHAT'S IN THE INK?

Black ink is just black color, right? Do this experiment to find out if there is more to black ink than you imagined.

SUPPLIES

* ✳ coffee filter
* ✳ scissors
* ✳ tape
* ✳ 2 clear glasses or jars
* ✳ 2 pencils
* ✳ 2 different kinds of black markers

1 Cut the coffee filter into two long strips that fit into the glasses.

2 Tape the end of each strip to the middle of a pencil. Make sure each strip hangs so the bottom of it is close to the bottom of each glass when you lay the pencil across the top of the glass.

3 Using one black marker, draw a line about an inch from the bottom of the strip. Do the same with the other marker and the other strip.

4 Pour water into the bottom of each glass, well below the ink lines.

5 Lay the pencil across the top of each glass. The bottom of each strip should be touching the water. Wait while the water moves up the strip. What do you see as the water moves up the strip?

WHAT'S HAPPENING? Different inks are made from different compounds. As the water moves up the strip, the water carries the compounds that make up black ink along with it. What do you notice about each color? Do some travel farther than others?

PROJECT!

CHEMICAL HUNT

SUPPLIES

✱ science journal and pencil

Chemicals are all around us. See how many you can find. Good places to look include the medicine cabinet, kitchen, and cleaning closet.

Warning: Ask an adult to help when handling any chemicals.

Object	Chemical found	What is It? (element, compound, mixture, solution)	Other names/ formulas for chemical

1 Start a chart like the one shown above in your science journal.

2 Look around your house for chemicals. Good places to start are the kitchen and bathroom. Ask an adult's permission before handling any chemicals. Read the product labels on the containers to check for chemicals.

3 Record your findings in your science journal. Include the name of the product and what chemicals it contains. What kind of chemical is it? A compound? A mixture? A mixture of compounds?

4 Try to figure out the chemical name or formula for the chemicals you find.

TRY THIS: Chances are you found some scary-sounding chemicals. With an adult's permission, look up some of those chemicals on the Internet. What are they? What are they used for?

OUT OF THE MIX

Mixtures can be separated into their original parts. It's easy to separate the colors of jelly beans, but what about a mixture of iron (Fe) and aluminum (Al) shavings? How do you separate them? What do you know about their physical properties? Iron is magnetic. Aluminum is not. How could you use a magnet to separate the two? There are many other ways mixtures can be separated, including grinding, filtering, melting, and boiling. It all depends on the properties of the elements in the mix.

Did You Know?

Sand contains grains of many different materials. The most common material in sand is silicon dioxide (SiO_2).

PROJECT!
FINDING THE SOLUTION

Can you tell the difference between a mixture and a solution? How about a suspension and a colloid? A suspension is a mixture made up of particles of a solid within a liquid that settle to the bottom if the mixture is left to sit for a while. When the particles are bigger than those in a solution but smaller than those in a suspension, these particles form colloids. In a colloid, these particles never separate. They stay suspended, which makes the mixture murky or opaque. Colloids in the kitchen include milk, gelatin, and marshmallows. Smoke, fog, and mist are all colloids in the air.

SUPPLIES

* science journal and pencil
* 5 clear glasses
* filtered or purified water
* ½ tablespoon each of baking soda, sugar, oatmeal, and olive oil
* 2 or 3 drops food coloring
* liquid measuring cup
* 5 spoons for stirring
* flashlight

1 Start a chart like the one below in your science journal.

Substance	Hypothesis Will make...	Observations (clear, murky, etc.)	Conclusion
baking soda			
sugar			
oatmeal			
olive oil			
food coloring			

WORDS TO KNOW

opaque: unable to be seen through.

2 Make a hypothesis as to what each of the substances will make when added to water. Will it be a mixture or a solution? What kind of mixture?

3 Pour ¼ cup water in each glass. Add one substance to each glass. Stir well. Be sure to use a different spoon for each glass.

4 Observe each glass. What do you see? Can you see clearly through the liquid? Does it look opaque? Can you see actual particles? Do any particles settle on the bottom? Try shining a flashlight through the side of the glass. Does this light change what you see?

5 Based on what you see and what you know about mixtures and solutions, write down your conclusions.

TRY THIS: With the help of an adult, find some other substances to test. Mix them in water. What kind of mixture or solution do you get?

WHAT HAPPENS WHEN COBALT, RADON AND YTTRIUM GET TOGETHER?

They get CoRnY!

CHAPTER 5

CHANGEABLE MATERIALS

There are all types of materials out there. Some are squishy. Others are hard. Some bend. Others break. Some are solid, some are liquid, some are a gas. Why does matter act in different ways? How can matter change so much?

You learned in the introduction to this book that matter has three states. A solid has its own shape that doesn't easily change. Its volume stays the same. A liquid takes the shape of its container. Its volume doesn't change either. A gas only has a shape when it's in a container. Its volume changes to fit what holds it.

? INVESTIGATE!

What would the world be like if matter could stay in only one state, such as a solid, liquid, or gas, and never change?

THE STATE OF A SILVER SPOON

The periodic table tells us the state of each element at room temperature. Elements can also change their states. They can go from solid to liquid to gas and back again.

For example, silver is solid at room temperature. Silver is used to make coins, jewelry, and many other things. You can use a silver spoon to scoop cereal or soup from a bowl. It's a solid that holds its shape.

To make a silver spoon, you start with a lump of raw silver. You need to heat the silver with special equipment to get it to 1,763.2 degrees Fahrenheit (961.78 degrees Celsius). That's very hot! This is silver's melting point. At this temperature, silver turns into a liquid. It flows easily and takes the shape of its container.

Next, you would pour liquid silver into a spoon mold. The liquid silver fills this shape. Then, let the silver cool. The silver turns back into a solid at its freezing point. When it's solid again, the silver will be in the shape of the mold. It will be a silver spoon.

During the spoon-making process, the chemical makeup of the silver doesn't change. The silver atoms stay the same. Why is it solid at one point and liquid at another?

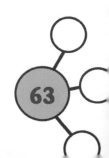

vibrate: to move back and forth very quickly.

WORDS TO KNOW

JIGGLE AND ZOOM

Materials made of molecules can change state from solid to liquid to gas and back. They can do this because of the way atoms move.

You can't see it, but atoms and molecules are always moving. Even in that solid silver spoon, the atoms are vibrating.

Atoms in a solid don't move very much. They just jiggle a little. In a liquid, the atoms have more energy. They move around more and slide past each other. Atoms have the most energy in a gas. They jiggle, zoom around, and even bump off each other.

For example, water is made of water molecules. Liquid water is water. Water put in a freezer turns into ice, the solid form of water. When water boils, it turns into steam, the gas form of water. The water molecules don't change. Instead, the way they move and the way they are packed together changes.

WATER BREAKS THE MOLD

Frozen water breaks the mold! What do ice cubes do in a glass of water? Do they float or sink? Ice expands when it freezes, making it less dense than liquid water. This makes water very unusual! Most materials are more dense in their solid state than in their liquid state.

You can think of atoms and the different states of matter this way. If you're hugging someone tightly, you're like two molecules in a solid. You're packed closely together and you can't really move around much.

SOLID
(TIGHTLY PACKED)

LIQUID
(LOOSELY CONNECTED)

GAS
(NEAR EACH OTHER)

If you're holding hands, you're sort of connected, like a liquid. You can move around and slide past each other, but you always stay an arm's length apart.

If you're not touching each other and dancing around, you're like two gas molecules. Maybe you'll move far apart, maybe closer together, maybe you'll even bump into each other.

Usually, the volume of a material changes as it changes state. Solids, where the molecules are tightly packed together, are usually the densest state. Density is a measure of how tightly items are packed together. A liquid, where molecules are moving around more, tends to be less dense than a solid. In a gas, the molecules move around even more. Materials tend to have the lowest density as a gas.

evaporation: the process in which matter changes from a liquid state to a gas state.

sublimation: the process in which matter changes from a solid to a gas without going through a liquid state.

WORDS TO KNOW

CHANGING STATES

Have you ever watched an ice cube on a hot day? It slowly melts into a puddle of water. Wait long enough and the puddle evaporates, leaving nothing behind.

Evaporation happens when matter changes state from a liquid to a gas. Adding heat to the process speeds it up. A heavy rain leaves behind puddles on the ground. Over time, the puddles dry up. The ground looks as if the puddles were never there. The puddles go away more quickly on a sunny day, because heat makes atoms move faster and jiggle farther away from each other. So the liquid changes into a gas.

Adding heat causes most materials to change from solid to liquid and eventually to gas. Sometimes, materials skip the middle state. They go straight from the solid state to the gas state. This is called sublimation.

IF H_2O IS WATER, WHAT IS H_2O_4?

Drinking, washing, and swimming in!

Water sometimes sublimates. You might have seen sublimation happening at home. Have you ever left an ice cube tray untouched in your freezer for weeks? If so, you may have noticed the ice cubes got smaller. Some of the ice molecules sublimated—they turned to gas and went into the air.

allotrope: one of two or more physical forms that an element can take.

WORDS TO KNOW

ALLOTROPES

What do pencil tips have in common with diamonds? Pencil tips are made from graphite. Both diamond and graphite are made up of only carbon atoms. Diamond and graphite are called **allotropes**. They are elements that contain all the same atoms, but they have very different physical properties.

A carbon atom is missing four electrons. Bonding with another carbon atom fills its valence shell. Remember, this is what they need to be happy. Carbon atoms tend to make large strings of carbon bonds and create different kinds of material. Carbon even has an allotrope that is shaped like a soccer ball! This is C_{60}, or buckminsterfullerene. **You can find out more about the different carbon structures at this website.**

KEYWORD PROMPTS

chemical carbon 🔍

Not only do molecules change when you add and take away heat, they also change from combining together chemically. In the next chapter, you'll learn about different chemical reactions that can happen when certain molecules mix together in certain ways!

? CONSIDER AND DISCUSS!

It's time to consider and discuss: What would the world be like if matter could stay in only one state, such as a solid, liquid, or gas, and never change?

PROJECT!
STATES IN A BAG

SUPPLIES

* 3 snack size zip-top plastic bags
* unpopped popcorn kernels, beans, or other small objects

In solids, molecules don't move around much. Molecules in a liquid move more. They slide around each other. Molecules in a gas move a lot! They move every which way. In this activity, we'll mimic molecules in the different states.

1 Fill one plastic bag full of kernels or your other small objects.

2 Fill the second bag one-third to half full of kernels.

3 Put just a few kernels in the third bag. Close each bag.

4 Shake each bag. Move the kernels around. Notice how the kernels move. Think about what you know of the states of matter. Which bag acts like a solid? Which acts like a liquid? Which acts like a gas? Record your findings in your science journal.

TRY THIS: Use a different type of material. Use something with smaller particles, such as sand, or something larger, such as dried kidney beans. How do the different objects act the same? How are they different? What does this mean for molecules and their states of matter?

Did You Know?

Diamonds form under extreme heat and pressure. These conditions are found only about 100 miles under the ground.

PROJECT!

FROZEN

A material's molecules don't change when it changes state. The molecules might move around more or less, but when a material returns to the state it started in, it should be exactly the same. Let's test this out.

SUPPLIES

* clear plastic cup or bottle
* water
* plastic wrap and rubber band, if using a cup
* permanent marker
* freezer

1 Fill a clear cup or bottle halfway with water and put the cap on the bottle. If using a cup, cover it with plastic wrap. Hold the plastic wrap in place with a rubber band.

2 Mark the waterline with a permanent marker on the outside of the bottle or cup.

3 Place the cup in the freezer. Check it every few hours.

4 Remove the cup from the freezer when the water is frozen. Mark the waterline. Is it different from the original waterline?

5 Leave the cup at room temperature. Allow the ice to melt.

6 When the ice is fully melted, check the waterline. Is it different from the original?

TRY THIS: Using two cups, put fresh water in one and salt water in the other. What happens? What happens if you add more or less salt to the salt water? What if you try sugar water?

PROJECT!

HOW SLOW CAN IT GO?

SUPPLIES

- science journal and pencil
- 4 test tubes, glasses, or jars
- 4 different liquids such as water, cooking oil, liquid dish soap, and honey
- timer
- 4 small marbles

Viscosity is a measure of how much a liquid resists flowing. This activity will compare the viscosities of a few different liquids.

1 Start a chart like the one shown below in your science journal.

Liquid	Hypothesis rank slowest-fastest (1–4)	Time	Actual rank slowest-fastest
water			
cooking oil			
dish detergent			
honey			

2 Make a hypothesis that ranks the liquids from slowest (1) to fastest (4). The slowest liquid will have the highest viscosity.

WORDS TO KNOW

viscosity: a measure of how much a liquid resists flowing.

3 Fill each test tube or glass with a different liquid. Make sure the liquids all go up to the same height in your containers.

4 For each liquid, drop the marble from the top of the test tube. Using the timer, time how long it takes for the marble to drop to the bottom. Be sure to drop each marble from the same height, and be ready to quickly start and stop the timer.

5 Based on the times you observed, rank the liquids from slowest (1) to fastest (4). How did your actual results vary from what you expected?

TRY THIS: With an adult's permission, find some other liquids to test. What is the slowest (highest viscosity) liquid you can find?

SLOW AS TAR PITCH

Tar pitch is the slowest-moving liquid in the world. Several scientists have tried to measure the viscosity of this thick liquid. Scientists set up the liquid to flow, and then they wait. And wait. And wait. The liquid is so slow it takes 7 to 13 years to form a single drop. It may take another 60 years or so for that drop to fall. The fall itself only takes about one-tenth of a second.

CHAPTER 6

GETTING A REACTION

What do rusting metal and exploding fireworks have in common? They're both chemical reactions! Sometimes, when molecules join together, they react with each other in a chemical reaction. Luckily, it's not always an explosive experience.

The chemicals that change during a reaction are the reactants. During a chemical reaction, bonds between atoms break and new bonds form. In the end, the same atoms exist, but they are grouped differently. They form new chemicals. The new chemicals are the reaction's products.

 INVESTIGATE!

What are some chemical reactions that happen every day? How are they useful?

REACTION OR NOT?

reactant: a substance involved in and changed by a chemical reaction.

product: a substance created by a chemical reaction.

WORDS TO KNOW

Sometimes, it's easy to know when a chemical reaction has occurred. For example, when sodium comes in contact with chlorine gas, it burns and glows. After the chemical reaction, there is no longer metal and gas. There is table salt.

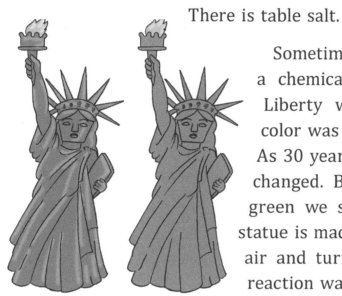

Sometimes, it's hard to recognize a chemical reaction. The Statue of Liberty was finished in 1886. Its color was brown, similar to a penny. As 30 years went by, the color slowly changed. By 1916, it was the bluish green we see today. The copper the statue is made of reacted with rain and air and turned a greenish color! The reaction was very slow, which made it hard to tell it was happening.

At first glance, some mixtures seem like reactions. When sugar mixes in water, it disappears. It is no longer white sugar crystals and clear water. It is now a sweet liquid. Isn't this a chemical reaction? No—the sugar can be removed from the water. If you left the glass of sugar water on your counter for several days, the water would evaporate and leave the sugar behind.

Did You Know?

A reaction changes the reactants. The products are new chemicals. It would take another reaction to get the reactants back.

SPEED IT UP!

Sodium and chlorine react quickly. Copper reacts with air and rain very slowly. The speed at which a reaction takes place is called the rate of reaction. There are ways to change a reaction's speed.

Molecules react when they come into contact with other molecules. If there are more molecules in a substance, there will be more chances for them to react. The number of molecules in the matter is the concentration.

The higher the concentration, the faster the rate of reaction. What if you want a slower reaction? What should you do to the concentration?

FROM FIREWORKS TO ROCKETS

Every Fourth of July, all across the United States, Americans celebrate with large fireworks displays. Each boom and color display is the result of a different chemical reaction. Fireworks have been around for more than 1,000 years. Different chemicals were added to the explosion to make them more impressive. The Chinese have used rockets to shoot off their fireworks for hundreds of years. **To read more about the relationship between fireworks and rockets, go to this NASA website.**

KEYWORD PROMPTS

NASA fireworks rockets 🔍

surface area: a measure of the amount of a material that is on the surface of the material.

endothermic: a process during which heat is absorbed.

WORDS TO KNOW

Another way to increase concentration is to increase surface area. In a solid, molecules on the surface are more likely to come in contact with other molecules. Breaking up the solid increases the surface area. Have you ever put sugar cubes in your hot tea? They take longer to dissolve than a spoonful of sugar because they have less surface area touching the hot liquid.

Adding heat is another way to increase the rate of reaction. Hotter molecules move more. The more they move, the more likely they are to collide. What should you do to the temperature to slow down the reaction?

HOT AND COLD

Imagine placing a bowl of ice in a sunny spot. Before long, the bowl is full of water and the area around the bowl is cool. What's going on?

Ice takes the energy from the sun's heat. This causes a change in the state of matter. The ice takes in more energy than it gives off. This makes it feel cold. Processes that use more energy than they make are called endothermic. Melting ice is a physical change instead of a chemical one. The material changes state, while the molecules stay the same.

WORDS ⊕ **KNOW**

exothermic: a process during which heat is given off.

Chemical reactions can also be endothermic. Have you ever used an instant ice pack from a first aid kit? When you punch the pack, a bag inside the pack breaks and releases chemicals. These chemicals interact with other chemicals in the pack. This reaction is endothermic. It absorbs energy. The pack gets cold and feels great against whatever hurts.

What happens when an adult strikes a match? The tip bursts into flame and the air around the match feels hot. This is a chemical reaction that gives off more energy than it uses. This is an exothermic reaction.

Physical changes can also be exothermic. Energy needs to be removed from a liquid in order for it to change into a solid. When you put water in the freezer, the freezer takes away the heat from the water. Eventually, it turns into ice.

Have you ever felt the air that comes from the fan on a freezer? It is warm. The process of turning liquids into solids gives off heat.

Did You Know?

Sweat helps keep us cool because the process of water evaporating from our skin is endothermic. Heat from the air is absorbed by the water on our skin and it turns into a gas.

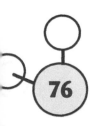

activation energy: the energy needed to start a reaction.

WORDS TO KNOW

MAKING IT HAPPEN

All reactions need a little bit of energy to get them started. This is called the activation energy. Some reactions get enough energy from two molecules bumping into each other. Others need a little help getting started.

Sometimes, all the molecules need is a little heat. The heat makes the molecules move faster, kicking off the reaction.

For example, hydrogen gas and oxygen gas are happy on their own. By sharing their electrons, the hydrogen in the H_2 molecules have filled their valence shells. The oxygen molecules in O_2 have also shared electrons to fill their valence shells.

However, if a lit match comes in contact with these gases, an explosion happens! The bonds break. The atoms reform as water molecules. The match supplied the energy needed to start the reaction.

Atoms and molecules are everywhere. They make up everything in our world. They are constantly changing. They might rearrange themselves to change their properties or combine with other atoms or molecules to form new substances altogether. Scientists are always finding new ways to put atoms together to make new materials. Maybe that will be you one day.

? **CONSIDER AND DISCUSS!**

It's time to consider and discuss: What are some chemical reactions that happen every day? How are they useful?

PENNY CHEMISTRY

Sometimes, chemical reactions are used to clean products. In this activity, we'll investigate the best way to clean a penny using what we know about atoms and molecules chemistry.

1 Using pieces of masking tape, label each cup: "Water," "Salt water," "Water and baking soda," "Vinegar," "Vinegar and salt." Prepare a piece of paper towel for each cup. Mark a spot R for rinsed. Mark another spot NR for not rinsed.

2 Fill the cups with the following substances. Use different measuring cups and measuring spoons for each substance, or clean and dry them after measuring each one. Be sure to stir each mixture well. Use a different stirrer for each cup.

Caution: Do not mix vinegar and baking soda!

- ¼ cup water

- ¼ cup water + 1 teaspoon salt

- ¼ cup water + 1 teaspoon baking soda

- ¼ cup vinegar

- ¼ cup vinegar + 1 teaspoon salt

3 Place two pennies in each cup. Set the timer for 5 minutes.

4 When the timer goes off, remove the pennies from each cup. Place one in the not-rinsed spot. Rinse the other penny under running water. Place that penny in the rinsed spot.

5 Which solution did the best job cleaning the penny? Which did the worst job?

6 Let the pennies sit overnight. Have any of the pennies changed in appearance?

WHAT'S HAPPENING? Vinegar is an **acid**, and acids react with metals. The acid solutions break down the copper oxide on the pennies. Once exposed, the copper can react again. The non-rinsed pennies may oxidize like the Statue of Liberty. You may see a bluish-green crust begin to form.

TRY THIS! Try other acids from the pantry, such as lemon juice or hot pepper sauce, to clean pennies. Do either of them work? Can you think of any other substances to try?

Caution: Ask an adult before you try any new substances.

WORDS TO KNOW

acid: a substance that loses hydrogen ions, also known as protons in water. Acids can accept a pair of electrons. Examples include lemon juice and vinegar.

PROJECT!

BAKING SODA POPPER

Caution: This activity packs a pop. You'll want to do it in a large bowl, the sink, or outside. This is an opportunity to observe a chemical reaction in action!

SUPPLIES

* white vinegar
* liquid measuring cup
* water
* measuring spoons
* zip-top sandwich bag
* snack bag or second zip-top sandwich bag
* scissors
* baking soda

1 Measure ¼ cup vinegar in the liquid measuring cup. Add 2 tablespoons warm water.

2 Cut the top off the second bag so it fits completely inside the zip-top bag, but keep it out for the moment.

3 Place ½ tablespoon baking soda in the cut-off bag.

4 Pour the liquid in the zip-top sandwich bag.

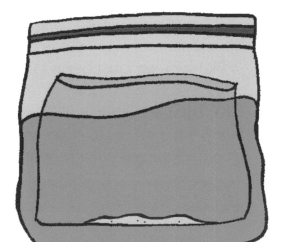

5 Place the baking soda bag into the sandwich bag. Keep the baking soda bag upright and be very careful not to spill the baking soda into the liquid. Squeeze the air out of the bags. Close the zip-top sandwich bag tightly.

6 Standing by the bowl or sink, shake the bag to release the baking soda into the vinegar-water solution.

7 Place the bag in the bowl or sink. Watch and listen! What happens?

8 Change one of the ingredients in some way. For example, you can change the amount of the ingredient or leave it out completely. What happens? What happens when you change the water temperature? Be sure to change only one thing at a time. Write down what you changed and how it changed the reaction.

WHAT'S HAPPENING?

Vinegar and baking soda react in a chemical reaction. One product is carbon dioxide (CO_2) gas. The gas fills the bag.

Did You Know?

When you increase the pressure on something, the molecules are squeezed closer together. When molecules are closer, they are more likely to run into each other. Increased pressure can start a chemical reaction.

PROJECT!

SWEET REACTION

Look at the reaction that made our baking soda popper pop. We mixed vinegar and baking soda. When the reaction ended, we were left with sodium acetate, carbon dioxide, and water. Let's use gumdrop models to see this reaction in action.

1 Choose a different color for each of the following elements: oxygen (O), hydrogen (H), carbon (C), and sodium (Na). Write down your key in your science journal.

2 Create gumdrop models for vinegar, which is acetic acid (CH_3COOH), and baking soda, which is sodium bicarbonate ($NaHCO_3$).

3 During the reaction, the bonds break and reform. Replace the H that's connected to the O in the acetic acid with the Na from the sodium bicarbonate.

4 Add the spare H from the acetic acid to an OH from the sodium bicarbonate to form H_2O.

5 Reposition the remaining atoms to form CO_2.

THINK ABOUT IT: It takes energy for you to break apart the old molecule models and form the new ones. How is this similar to what happens during a chemical reaction?

ELEMENTAL MAD LIB

Pick up a pencil and get a friend or two to explore the ideas in this book by filling out this silly Mad Lib.

- **noun:** a person, place, or thing
- **plural noun:** more than one person, place, or thing
- **adjective:** a word that describes a noun
- **verb:** an action word
- **adverb:** a word that describes a verb

Mind Your Elements

There once was an _____ who went by the name of _____. _____
⎯⎯ NOUN ⎯⎯   NOUN-NAME   NAME

always dreamed of turning _____ into _____. _____ enlisted his
⎯⎯⎯⎯⎯⎯⎯ NOUN   ELEMENT   NAME

assistant, _____, to help.
        PERSON IN THE ROOM

_____ took _____ _____, mixed them together, and brought them
  NAME   NUMBER   PLURAL NOUN

to their _____. Then he told the assistant to add _____.
        NOUN   ANOTHER ELEMENT

All the _____ looked similar. The assistant added _____ instead.
     PLURAL NOUN   ANOTHER ELEMENT

The _____ started glowing and fizzing. It gave off an _____ _____ that
   NOUN   ADJECTIVE   NOUN

seemed like lightning.

"What did you do?" yelled _____ as he tried to stop the _____ _____.
                       NAME   ADJECTIVE   NOUN

When the _____ cooled down to a _____, they looked at the _____.
       NOUN   NOUN   NOUN

It was quite _____ and had a _____ _____. It definitely wasn't
          ADJECTIVE   COLOR   NOUN

_____, but it had a high _____.
FIRST ELEMENT   NOUN

"Oh well," _____ said. "At least it makes a good _____."
        NAME   NOUN

A

abbreviation: a short form of a word.

acid: a substance that loses hydrogen in water. Acids can accept a pair of electrons. Examples include lemon juice and vinegar.

activation energy: the energy needed to start a reaction.

allotrope: one of two or more physical forms that an element can take.

atom: a very small piece of matter. Atoms are the tiny building blocks that make up everything in the universe.

atomic: about or relating to atoms.

atomic number: the number of protons in an atom's nucleus.

atomic weight: the average weight of an atom in an element.

attract: a force that pulls things closer, usually applied to a magnet.

B

boiling point: the temperature at which a liquid boils.

bond: a force that holds atoms together.

brittle: describes something that can be easily broken or snapped.

C

charge: a force of electricity that can be either positive or negative.

chemical: a substance that has certain features that can react with other substances.

chemical reaction: the action that occurs between atoms or molecules to form one or more new substances.

chemistry: the science of how atoms and molecules combine to form substances and how those substances interact, combine, and change.

clockwise: the direction that follows the hands of a clock.

compound: a substance made up of two or more elements.

concentration: the amount of a substance in relation to others.

conductor: a material through which electricity and heat move easily.

conduct: to act as the channel through which something travels.

core: the middle part of something.

counterclockwise: the direction that goes opposite to the hands of a clock.

covalent bond: a chemical bond where atoms share electrons.

D

density: a measure of how closely packed items are.

dissolve: to mix with a liquid and become part of the liquid.

double bond: a covalent bond where two pairs of electrons are shared.

ductile: describes something that can be hammered thin or drawn out into a wire without breaking.

E

electrical current: the flow of electrons through a material.

electron: a particle in an atom with a negative charge that moves around the nucleus.

element: a substance whose atoms are all the same. Examples include gold, oxygen, nitrogen, and carbon.

endothermic: a process during which heat is absorbed.

evaporation: the process in which matter changes from a liquid state to a gas state.

exothermic: a process during which heat is given off.

F

freezing point: the temperature at which a liquid turns into a solid.

G

gas: one of the three states of matter. The particles in a gas are not bound to each other and move very fast in all directions. A gas does not have a definite shape or volume.

gravity: the force that pulls objects toward each other and holds you on the earth.

group: all elements in one column of the periodic table.

H

heterogeneous mixture: a mixture where particles are not evenly spread out.

homogeneous mixture: a mixture where all particles are evenly distributed.

I

infinite: with no limit, going on forever.

insulator: a material that prevents heat, sound, or electricity from passing through it easily.

ion: an atom that has a positive or negative charge.

ionic bond: a chemical bond formed between ions of opposing charges.

L

Lewis dot diagram: a diagram that shows the bonding between atoms, in a molecule in which dots represent valence electrons.

liquid: one of the three states of matter. The particles in a liquid cluster together and flow. A liquid has a definite volume, but takes the shape of its container.

M

mass: the amount of material that an object contains.

matter: anything that takes up space.

medium: the material artists use to create their art, such as crayons, paint, and ink. Plural is media.

melting point: the temperature at which a solid melts.

metal: an element that is hard, shiny material. It conducts heat and electricity and can be melted.

metalloid: an element that has both metal and nonmetal properties.

mixture: a mix of two or more substances that are not chemically bonded together.

molecule: a group of atoms bound together to form matter.

N

neutral: having no charge.

neutron: a particle in the nucleus of an atom that has no charge.

nonmetal: an element that does not have the properties of a metal.

nucleus: the core of an atom.

O

opaque: unable to be seen through.

P

palette: a board used by a painter for layering and mixing paint colors.

period: all elements in one row of the periodic table.

periodic table: the chart that shows and organizes all the known elements.

pointillism: a style of art that uses tiny dots of color to create an image.

polygon: a closed shape, made with all straight lines.

product: a substance created by a chemical reaction.

property: a special quality of a substance.

proton: a particle in the nucleus of an atom that has a positive charge.

Q

quark: a particle that makes up neutrons and protons.

R

radioactive: describes an atom whose nucleus can break down, forming a different kind of atom.

rate of reaction: the speed with which a chemical reaction takes place.

ratio: the relationship in size or quantity between two things.

reactant: a substance involved in and changed by a chemical reaction.

repel: a force that pushes away.

S

shell: the distance at which an electron moves around the nucleus.

solid: one of the three states of matter. The particles in a solid are bound together tightly. A solid has a definite shape and volume and does not flow.

solute: a substance that dissolves into another to make a solution.

solution: the result when one substance has dissolved into another.

solvent: a substance that can dissolve other substances.

state of matter: the form that matter takes. There are three common states of matter: solid, liquid, and gas.

strong force: the force between particles in an atom's nucleus.

sublimation: the process in which matter changes from a solid to a gas without going through a liquid state.

substance: matter, the material that something is made of.

surface area: a measure of the amount of a material that is on the surface of the material.

T

tan: one of the seven polygons that makes up a tangram.

V

valance electrons: the electrons in an atom's outermost shell.

vibrate: to move back and forth very quickly.

viscosity: a measure of how much a liquid resists flowing.

volume: the amount of space an object takes up.

W

weight: a measure of the force of gravity on an object.

METRIC CONVERSIONS

Use this chart to find the metric equivalents to the English measurements in this book. If you need to know a half measurement, divide by two. If you need to know twice the measurement, multiply by two. How do you find a quarter measurement? How do you find three times the measurement?

English	Metric
1 inch	2.5 centimeters
1 foot	30.5 centimeters
1 yard	0.9 meter
1 mile	1.6 kilometers
1 pound	0.5 kilogram
1 teaspoon	5 milliliters
1 tablespoon	15 milliliters
1 cup	237 milliliters

BOOKS

Oh, Ick! 114 Science Experiments Guaranteed to Gross You Out by Joy Masoff (Workman Publishing, 2016).

Burn: Michael Faraday's Candle by Darcy Pattison (Mims House, 2016).

Who Was Marie Curie? by Megan Stine (Grosset & Dunlap, 2014).

WEBSITES

Chem4Kids: chem4kids.com/files/atom_intro.html

Jefferson Lab: education.jlab.org/itselemental

Royal Society of Chemistry: www.rsc.org/periodic-table

Los Alamos National Laboratory: periodic.lanl.gov

A Science Odyssey: pbs.org/wgbh/aso/tryit/atom

Quarked!: quarked.org

Science Kids: sciencekids.co.nz/sciencefacts/chemistry.html

Molecularium: nanospace.molecularium.com

University of Colorado: phet.colorado.edu/en/simulations/category/chemistry

Discovery of Graphene: graphene.manchester.ac.uk/explore/the-story-of-graphene

Zoom: pbskids.org/zoom/activities/sci

RESOURCES

MUSEUMS

The Museum of Science and Industry in Chicago:
msichicago.org/explore/whats-here/exhibits/science-storms/the-exhibit/atoms

Children's Museum of Houston: cmhouston.org

Manhattan Project National Historic Park: nps.gov/mapr

The Sterling Hill Mining Museum: sterlinghillminingmuseum.org/periodictable

QR CODE GLOSSARY

Page 3: exploratorium.edu/ronh/weight

Page 10: etc.usf.edu/clipart/galleries/780-tangrams

Page 29: aip.org/history/exhibits/curie/periodic.htm

Page 35: periodic.lanl.gov

Page 35: education.jlab.org/itselemental

Page 35: www.rsc.org/periodic-table

Page 44: chemheritage.org/historical-profile/gilbert-newton-lewis

Page 52: polychem.mat.ethz.ch/outreach/Thelargestsyntheticmolecule.html

Page 67: chemicool.com/elements/carbon.html

Page 74: grc.nasa.gov/WWW/K-12/TRC/Rockets/history_of_rockets.html

ESSENTIAL QUESTIONS

Introduction: If everything is made of atoms, why do things look and feel different from each other?

Chapter 1: What are the parts of an atom? Where are they found in the atom?

Chapter 2: Why is it important to keep information about the elements organized in a chart?

Chapter 3: How do atoms join together to make new chemicals?

Chapter 4: What is the difference between a mixture and a solution? How can you tell them apart?

Chapter 5: What would the world be like if matter could stay in only one state, such as a solid, liquid, or gas, and never change?

Chapter 6: What are some chemical reactions that happen every day? How are they useful?

88

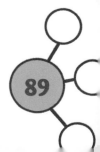